A World of Field Trips

Going to a Park

Rebecca Rissman

Heinemann Library
Chicago, Illinois

www.capstonepub.com
Visit our website to find out more information about Heinemann-Raintree books.

To order:
☎ Phone 888-454-2279
🖥 Visit www.capstonepub.com
to browse our catalog and order online.

© 2012 Heinemann Library
an imprint of Capstone Global Library, LLC
Chicago, Illinois

Edited by Rebecca Rissman, Dan Nunn, and Catherine Veitch
Designed by Richard Parker
Picture research by Tracy Cummins
Originated by Capstone Global Library Ltd
Printed and bound in China by Leo Paper Products Ltd

15 14 13 12 11
10 9 8 7 6 5 4 3 2 1

Library of Congress Cataloging-in-Publication Data
Rissman, Rebecca.
  Going to a park / Rebecca Rissman.
    p. cm.—(A world of field trips)
  Includes bibliographical references and index.
  ISBN 978-1-4329-6068-1 (hb)—ISBN 978-1-4329-6077-3
(pb) 1. School field trips—Juvenile literature. 2. Parks—Juvenile literature. I. Title.
  LB1047.R577 2012
  371.3'84—dc22   2011015152

Acknowledgments
We would like to thank the following for permission to reproduce photographs: Corbis pp. 10 (© Granger Wootz/Blend Images), 20, 23d (© Ocean): Getty Images pp. 8 (Caroline von Tuempling), 11 (Peter Macdiarmid), 15 (Dan Kitwood), 21 (blue jean images), 23b (Dan Kitwood; istockphoto p. 16 (© Daniel Bendjy); Shutterstock pp. 4 (© S Duffett©), 5 (BlueOrange Studio), 6 (© Jamie Wilson), 7 (© Inacio Pires), 9 (© Chee-Onn Leong), 12 (© Straga), 13 (© michaeljung), 14 (© Yarek Gora), 17 (© Cheryl Casey), 18 (© Twisted Shots), 19 (© Parkisland), 22 (© Dmitriy Shironosov), 23a (© Inacio Pires), 23c (© Parkisland).

Front cover photograph of children inline skating in a park reproduced with permission of Getty Images (Christopher Robbins). Back cover photograph of a girl on a tire swing reproduced with permission of Shutterstock (© Cheryl Casey).

Every effort has been made to contact copyright holders of any material reproduced in this book. Any omissions will be rectified in subsequent printings if notice is given to the publisher.

Contents

Field Trips .4

Field Trip to a Park 6

Different Parks 10

How Should You Act at a Park?. . . .20

What Do You Think? 22

Picture Glossary. 23

Index .24

Field Trips

People take field trips to visit
new places.

People take field trips to see
new things.

Field Trip to a Park

Some people take field trips
to parks.

A park is a special outdoor place.

Some parks are places where people can look at animals.

Some parks are places where people can sit on a sunny day.

Different Parks

Some parks are in big cities.

You can go for a boat ride. Always
go with an adult.

Some parks are in the country.

You can play sports on the grass.

Some parks have special gardens.

You can walk through this maze
made of plants!

Some parks have playgrounds.

You can swing on this tire swing.

Some parks are near old castles or homes.

sculpture

You can see very old sculptures.

How Should You Act at a Park?

Wear sunscreen when you play in a park on a sunny day.

Always throw your trash in a
trash can.

What Do You Think?

What can you do in this park?

Look on page 24 for the answer.

Picture Glossary

 **maze** set of paths. Some plant mazes are big enough to walk through.

 **park** special outdoor area that is meant for people to enjoy

 **sculpture** type of art that an artist carves or makes out of a material such as stone, wood, or clay

 **sunscreen** special cream that helps block the Sun. Always wear sunscreen when you are out in the Sun.

Index

animals 8

boat 11

gardens 14

maze 15, 23

playgrounds 16

sculptures 19, 23

sports 7

Notes to Parents and Teachers

Before reading
Explain to children that a field trip is a short visit to a new place, and that it often takes place during a school day. Ask children if they have ever taken a field trip. Tell children that parks are special areas where people can rest, play, and see animals. Explain that there are many different types of parks.

After reading
- Review pages 20–21 on how to behave at a park. Ask children if they have any questions. Then take children to a local park to play. Afterwards, ask the children to write a story about their experience at the park.

Answer to page 22
You can play in this playground.